Analyze People: The revealing Power of Facial Expressions

How to read people accurately and spot any subtle social cues, repressed emotions or even potential deception via nonverbal behavior

By John C. Davis

Table of Content

Introduction

I want to thank you and congratulate you for downloading the book, Analyze people: The revealing power of facial expressions.

This book contains proven steps and strategies on how to analyze people with the aid of facial expressions.

Your ability to analyze people has a great impact on the manner in which you shall deal with them. As you get to understand the other person's feelings, you get to adapt your message and begin communicating in a way that yields the maximum results possible. This is also essential as it tends to avoid the possibility of causing chaos among the two of you.

Think of a situation where somebody is angry over a certain matter but manages to hide it. On your part, you are unaware of this anger issue and begin to make jokes around the same. As much as your friend could have kept you in the dark regarding the problem, you making fun of it could result into them being infuriated and eventually all that anger bursts out of them.

There are different strategies you could follow in analyzing people. You may decide to listen to their words, take a look at hand gestures or even analyze their facial expressions.

You may decide to pay attention to deviations (inconsistencies) in the gestures and words used by someone.

Of all of these strategies, facial expression seems to be the most effective one. Most people may device ways to control their words and actions, but they tend to have a difficulty controlling what their faces say.

The face simply never lies. It is similar to a little child lying to you that she hasn't taken candy but you can see sugary marks on their mouth.

Due to the amazing power of facial expressions to always reveal the truth, this book concentrates on helping you read someone's face and reveal the underlying truth in whatever they tell you. It aims at equipping you with this essential people-reading skill so that you are never deceived again. Whether you are dealing with your partner whom you suspect for cheating, or a work colleague who might have tried to undercut you in a deal, the people analysis skill will help you get your facts right. And even as you gain the skills to read other people, there are times you personally want to share a different message with the others while at the same time making sure that your facial expressions do not give you away. Maybe you want to encourage your child to face a particular matter but you personally have your doubts. It is important that you also have what it takes to manage your personal facial expressions. This book will show you how to do that.

Thanks again for downloading this book, I hope you enjoy it!

Chapter 1
The Essence of Analyzing People's Facial Expression

People are an open book. If you pay a keen attention to what they do and look at their facial expressions as they speak, you are likely to get a better picture of their attitudes and personalities. It is important to analyze people as this gives you an upper hand in different situations. This chapter demonstrates the different reasons as to why you should analyze people.

1.Helps strike healthy friendship

A common misconception about the analysis of people is that it may lead to trust issues. That is entirely untrue. When you make analysis of people prior to even becoming friends, you get to know them better and can thus form healthy friendships. You know their likes and dislikes, and can even tell if they are genuine or not. With these facts, individuals who know how to analyze people will always get into helpful and healthy friendships and relationships. You do not want to get into relationships and friendships that will lead you to being taken advantage of. The only way to guarantee that is not to just take in the words said by the other person but to also look at their facial expressions and tell whether the two agree.

2.Helps find a common ground

If you know how to analyze people, you can put that skill into arriving at a common ground. This is a skill that you will not just use with a few people. It can also be used while delivering vital speeches to various audiences. As you say something, you gauge what their reactions are through people analysis skill.

When you realize that you have gone too far, you can backtrack slightly so that you all get to a common understanding. Getting to a common understanding means being at a position that is neutral for both of you, hence chances of getting into confrontations are minimized.

3.Helps speak in a language understandable to your audience

When you know how to analyze people, you can tell when they understand what you are saying and when they don't. At such times, you can easily see when whatever you have been saying hasn't been understood, even if the other person doesn't tell you that. For example, as a teacher, you could see from your student's faces that they are lost and require proper clarification. Similarly, as a parent, you may give instructions to your children but that doesn't mean they will understand whatever you said right away.

Through the people analysis skills, you can gauge whether your communication style is being understood by the other person or whether you need to change your mode of message delivery.

4.Makes you dependable for advises

Your friends are bound to get into trouble from time and again with their boyfriends or girlfriends. Because you know how to analyze people, you can listen to their side of the story while analyzing them too and also get to interact with their partners before giving an advice. People tend to reveal more with their facial expressions. You can analyze these to get the hidden message behind their words.

The advises you give are more likely to be genuine and helpful. They are based on facts rather than assumptions, hence helpful to the person asking for your advice.

Even if your advice would not be followed to completion as you would have wanted, time will prove that you were right. That goes a long way in solidifying your position as a dependable person for advices.

5.*You are always prepared*

If you know how to analyze people, you will always be prepared for outcomes that would have otherwise been surprising. Whether you are getting ready for a meeting with the board of directors, or your juniors at work made a catastrophic mistake that they are trying to hide, you can analyze them and know it.

We live in a world where however possess information has the upper hand. When you analyze members of your team, you are able to collect the information without them even knowing it. In case they were planning anything that isn't favorable to you, you can undo it prior to its occurrence.

Let's say your boyfriend or girlfriend has been acting weirdly in recent days but they still tell you everything is fine. You could use your analysis skills to find out that they are actually cheating and even have plans to break up with you! They may think that their plans are well hidden but in real sense you already have the facts and just decided to play along. When they eventually decide to come out of the hiding and drop the bombshell, it won't be much of a bombshell to you.

6.It makes you more considerate

The fact that you analyze people gets you to understand why they may act in certain ways. You develop some sense of protection towards others, a protectionist behavior that the average person may not have.

If you are the boss at your workplace or in any other organization and conflicts are brought to you, you will want to first analyze the conflicting persons prior to decide. The ability to listen to all the people will not be motivated by you having too much time but by the desire to analyze all so that you do not end up making the wrong decision. During the analysis, important information is revealed to you like what would have actually made people to act in such and such a manner. Thus, as you start making the final decision, you will put all these facts into consideration.

This is in contradiction to individuals who make decisions based on what they hear. The decisions of such individuals could even be biased and may end up punishing the wrong person. As a person with people analysis skills, punishment is not within your scope because you know sometimes people act not out of their will but out of a background force. This force is only revealed to you when you analyze them.

7.You get really smart

Not to brag but knowing how to analyze people makes you really smart. From the many years of doing this, you wire your brains to think in a certain manner that the brains of other people do not. The process has also led you to know the many different types of people on our planet and can form topics that anchor well with these. You form well formulated opinions on topics and can't wait to speak them out. You are the kind of a person who can deliver an electrifying speech in different occasion with various audiences. All you have to do is analyze the audience and choose the direction in which your topic should move. Furthermore, the people analysis skills empower you to stimulate anyone's brain. Thinking, talking, discussing and conversing are your erogenous zones and anyone can tap into those in a stimulating way. Having understood the other person, you know what you can say to get them stimulated and what to avoid as it could lag them behind.

Chapter 2
Facial Communication for Personal Happiness

Effective facial expression communication skills are of benefit to any person at any stage of their life. These are the kinds of skills that are needed in personal life and in professional life as well. The constant reminder since childhood that you need to sharpen your communication skills wasn't in vain. That's because your elders at that time knew what communication skills can do for your life. Now that you are old enough, you should have a better understanding as to why facial communication is such a crucial issue in human relations.

Improving your ability to communicate with your facial expressions can tremendously benefit different spheres of your life. You should expect to increase your happiness, confidence and successful social interaction.

Enhance opportunities for personal growth

When you increase your ability to facially communicate effectively, you open up more avenues for your personal growth. People are happier when they have a sense of improvement rather than stagnation.

Individuals who have these strong communication skills have better leadership abilities including the motivation of family members at home or subordinates at work.

From the perspective of self-maintenance, the communication skills are essential in the management of stress. When you have good communication skills, you can properly share with your therapist whatever is bothering you and he/she will be able to help you accordingly.

Facial communication skills also make you assertive, meaning that you can effectively take charge of conversations or situations, bringing about meaningful conclusions. You do not want to keep revolving around a matter for too long as doing so is equivalent to wasting time, which has zero benefit to your personal growth.

With improved communication skills, you are able to meet a partner or make new friends. Due to the strong command on your communication, you carry yourself in a confident manner, attracting admiration from others. It allows you to project some gregarious and charismatic personality which most people love associating with. These advances in personal growth goes a long way in improving your networking skills, hence more opportunities for your social life and professional progression. The state of our world today requires you to have different kinds of connections in order to be more competitive. Your ability to ingratiate yourself with company top management may see you get more responsibilities, higher pay and increased chances to climb the social ladder.

Physical communication is comprised of facial expressions, hand gestures, fidgeting and eye movement, all of which constitute major parts of a communication. Many also consider this to be the hardest form of communication to monitor and control. People tend to be focused mainly on what they are hearing and saying such that they forget to pay attention to what their physical movements are saying. If you can be able to control that, you will have an upper hand in the conversation. This is something that an effective communicator is able to do and in the long run see their personal lives grow further.

With effective communication, you will be able to earn a diploma, find your dream job, master the art of persuasion, and increase your visibility and reach. All these factors are associated with personal growth and bring one immense happiness.

Listening to underlying needs

Talking of underlying needs, it is vital that you be able to identify these needs in others as well. During most negotiations, it is typical for people to commonly pay attention on the demands being made by the other side.

However, what they should actually focus on is the other person's unexpressed desires and underlying needs. Given that we all have unique needs, it is possible to satisfy several people without losing.

All you have to do is make use of your effective communication skills to understand the underlying needs involved and satisfy them.

Do not be hindered by what the other person is saying. Your concentration ought to be on the needs. What could be any happier ending in a negotiation than for all of you to end up at a win-win situation?

Imagine a situation where your family is planning a vacation. This is supposed to be a happy negotiation but you get into a deadlock as you can't seem to settle on the final vacation destination.

Your son wants to go to the Rocky Mountains while your spouse wants Texas. The differences may seem irreconcilable at the start but if you open up the communication lines and look beyond the demands, you will see that there are needs which can be met jointly. From gentle inquiry, you may realize that your wife just needs a place that is warm and has tennis facilities while your son just wants to see mountains. Having learnt this, you will be able to see that a resort in Colorado can meet these needs.

Effective communication for happy relationships

When you are happy in your relationship, you are bound to be happy overall.

Most of the times the sadness that surrounds our work life or relations with our friends can be associated directly with differences in our relationships. Many people tend to carry their arguments with their spouse to other spheres of their lives.

Thus, it is logical to conclude that if you can establish a happy relationship, you will be happier. That is achievable through healthy communication.

A healthy communication is a kind of communication in which you listen to your partner speak before responding accordingly. You do not engage in undue shouts against each other. Rather, you are patient enough to let the other finish telling their side of anything while you give them your undivided attention. Effective communicators know how to do so.

Always remember that listening is the most important communication skill in your relationship. As the other person is speaking, do not daydream or get lost into thinking about what to say next. When you listen, you will be able to give an appropriate feedback, making your partner happy and in the long run have a satisfactory relationship.

Chapter 3
How to tell If Someone is Faking a Facial Expression

In chapter 3, you will learn how to decode facial expressions but before that, it is paramount that you have a strong grasp on how people can hide these expressions. When you have this understanding, you are empowered to tell if someone is trying create different perceptions in your mind from what their words are saying. This chapter seeks to enlighten you on that.

Why people try to hide their facial expressions?

There are a number of reasons as to why people choose to hide their facial expressions. For some, it is a way suppressing their emotions towards a given matter. As much as their words portray a particular image in your brain, it is their wish that you do not get to see their actual emotions on the same subject. For example, you may be holding a conversation with a potential partner who likes you but they are afraid to let you know that – maybe because they are too shy or unwilling to be the first ones to reveal that. Because of their unwillingness to express their emotions, they could try to fake their facial expressions. In such a case, it is up to you to discover that on your own. You have to look closely at their faces as they speak to you so as to get their actual feelings. You never know if it could be the only thing that leads you finding one true love!

Some people have just too much ego that they wouldn't allow their facial expressions to be shown. When clearly a particular matter has hurt them and that they are undergoing immense pain in the inside, their big egos would not let them reveal such details. These are the kinds of people who suffer in silence and within a couple of days, you may get information that they did something more harmful – suicide for example.

There is also this category of people who hide their facial expressions, not because they want to do so, but because they just do not know how to solve negative emotions. As negativity builds up from the inside and starts to show in the face, they soon device ways to hide any form of negative expressions to lock you out from analyzing them. They want to look happy when in real sense they are sad. They want you to see that they are having a good time but in reality there is a sickness or school fees issue that has been stressing them for months now. We all know that negative emotions can lead to frowning on one's face, which essentially makes them not so approachable or appealing. Thus, in an attempt to retain their attractiveness, they conceal any form of negative facial expression which would have otherwise confronted them.

In other cases, some people may hide their facial expressions just so as to please. These are the people who believe in the philosophy that what you do not know cannot hurt you.

Their idea is that when they keep some information from you, you may still have a happy life. Thus, when they speak to you, they will struggle to build a certain kind of facial expression which conveys the message that all is well while in real sense that is further from the truth. Let's say for example one of your best friends gets some bad news from the doctor that they have cancer and that they have only a few years with you.

They love you so much and know how much such news could be devastating to you. In order to save you all the pain, they may choose to struggle with the pain on their own, believing that provided you do not know about it, you will have a happy life. Whenever they tell stories with you, they will do their best not to let you into the inside. From their facial expressions, they will be smiling for you whereas only they know the agony they are experiencing. You have the responsibility of decoding this so that you get the message they are trying to lock inside.

5 Signs someone is being fake: How to tell they are faking facial expressions

1.Taking deep breath

This is a technique that seems to be universal amongst all people who express untrue facial expressions. You will often see them appear to be unrelaxed and continuously breathe in and out heavily in the midst of their explanations over a matter you just asked. Because they know that for you to believe the facial expression they just wore to impress you, they have to appear calm. That is what the deep breathes are meant to do – take in more oxygen so that they can recollect their composure and be cool. If you are not keen enough on the breathing pattern, their faces may appear calm to you and succeed in the deception.

2. Putting up a fake smile

A smile never says that someone is happy at all times.
Someone who smiles and has a bubbly look on their face can win hearts and affection. As a result, many assume that with just the right smile, they will be able to hide their feelings like anger or sadness.

But a fake smile will always be fake. It may convince some people at the first glance but a keen individual will soon realize this smile is fake. How well you know the individual could guide you into distinguishing between the smile they just put up and their real happy smile.
But even if you do not know them that well, their inability to sustain the smile will eventually prove it fake.

3. Trying not to supporting the head

There is something about 'cooked' facial expressions that makes the head heavy. A droopy head held by the first of the hand or a sulky face buried into the palms can be giveaways of a gloomy mood, depression or sadness. People who understand the technique of hiding facial expressions know this. Thus, they always try to make sure that their head is held up high to better deceive you. When you are keen on them, there will be these occasions when they can no longer hold the head up and end up burying the face in their palms for some seconds before realizing that they may show you that they are lying. Careful analysis of the struggles not to support the head could reveal to you that they are faking their facial expression.

4. *Struggling to relax the face*

A relaxed face can easily build up a deceiving facial expression. For example, your son may have committed an offense in school and they come to report the matter to you, hoping to come out as victims. If your first glance on their faces shows them as being relaxed, you could actually be deceived and even get on the wrong side with the teachers. However, if you saw their faces were not relaxed even before they started the explanation, you can tell right away that there must be a problem somewhere. When you speak to someone and at one time their face is relaxed and at the other one it is not, that is a sign of a problem. Within a few minutes their face could be straight while at another it is steel and acting like a tough guy. This shows that they may have tried to relax it up to a certain point when they could do it no more. There is something here, take a deep look at their faces and you shall see it.

5. *Silent lip movements*

To be calm, some people speak to themselves. They may say something like "Calm down, you can do this. Just stay cool." If you are not careful, they may actually succeed in being calm and creating a falsified facial expression. Through a keen look at the lip movements, you may tell that the person has more things that they are hiding under their facial expressions.

Chapter 4
Decoding Facial Expressions

The universality of facial expression has been subject to debate ever since Darwin's time to date. Some facial expressions seem to be universal while others confined to particular zones. However, there are some expressions of the face which seem to be sending the same message among individuals from all corners of the world. This chapter decodes the hidden message in various facial expressions. This is an important factor because 80% of the emotions are shown and revealed on one's face.

Do not just listen to the words, pay attention to what the face says.

#1: Furrowed brow most often indicates to signs of discomfort

The furrowed brow facial expression accurately represents what it means to feel and create negative emotions. When one starts to get stressed, anxious or angry, their brow is furrowed. Even if the individual may pretend to be all happy around you, this is a great giveaway!

#2: Eye contact typically indicates interest and confidence

Typically, when someone is telling the truth, they tend to look you directly in the eyes. This is called eye contact.

Such individuals have immense confidence in whatever they are saying that they do not see the problem in facing you directly. When the speaker and the receiver maintain a direct and attentive eye contact, it could be translated that both parties are interested in the subject of discussion and that some level of truths are involved. One is also seen as being confident. The converse sends the message of shyness, lies or uninterested in all that's said.

#3: If the eyes are averted downwards, shame is probably involved

This is one of the most uniquely recognized facial expressions. In most cases, the eyes of the individuals are normally averted downward while the person wears a saddened and worried look. The head also takes a downward look, with a frowning or neutral mouth. In simpler terms, shame could be associated with submission. It's as if the individuals are sending the message that they have been caught when they least expected it and that they have no choice than to submit. For primates, when the dominant individual successfully forces the other side into submission, the losing side tend to look downward in submission.

In your observation of facial expressions, you will likely see shame in the other person's face. However, what you may not see is what cause that shame.

The shame could be due to something they did and didn't like it or they were involved in some competition and lost. These will be manifested in broad ways thus some background information would guide you in coming up with a more effective conclusion.

#4: If they repeatedly touch the face, they are probably nervous

There are many things that can make someone nervous. When an individual is faced with a situation likely to cause one anxious, you will notice them repeatedly touching their face.

One may be having financial problems or thinking of changing jobs and all these emotions will build up in them to a point they can no longer take it. When that happens, they tend to bury their face in their hands and take in deep breathes.

These symptoms of anxiety or nervousness can grow to a larger extent that your normal life is interfered with.

#5: If you see their mouth and eyes are wide open simultaneously, they may be surprised

Gaping mouth and widened eyes are the trademarks for a surprised look. Surprise or shock as an emotion is closely associated with fear. The face made by a surprised person is one that instinctively forms.

This occurs unconsciously to us and is triggered when something that we did not expect happens. When this unexpected event takes root, the eyes widen and the pupils expand so that they can cover more of the increased environment.

#6: Frowns and slanted eyebrows may display sad emotions being experienced

Unlike happiness, sadness assumes a less welcoming face. Many people find it easy to walk towards a happy person but will rarely have the same freedom when approaching a sad person. Sadness is facially expressed by a frown and slanted eyebrows. These are then coupled with feelings of loss and helplessness. Withdrawn individuals typically display this face. The expression originates in a simple manner: the features which show sadness are basically your usual facial features but in their reduced form. Everything tends to droop downward, but they seem not to be headed in any specific direction. It could as well be an indication of defeat, lack of initiative to engage others or giving up. Certain individuals couple the sadness facial expression with teary eyes (but this is not always a guarantee). One has to be careful when associating teary eyes with sadness because sometimes one could form tears as a result of too much joy.

#7: Clenched jaw or tightened neck shows stress

The two limbic responses are linked to the limbic system in the brain. The limbic system plays the crucial role of controlling how we react to threats, and display emotions.
When you notice someone miss the bus at stage, they will likely clench their jaws and rub their necks. Or the boss sends a letter to the staff that everyone will work over the weekend and all of a sudden the orbits of their eyes narrow as their chin lowers.

#8: Half-open eyelids and weak-looking shows tiredness

Half-open eyelids are the main facial expression that the person you are looking at is exhausted. In an attempt to stay awake, this person typically raises the eyebrows. When you perform too much of a task while allowing yourself no room for rest, fatigue soon kicks in. The face expresses this in a weak-like appearance, probably seeking sympathy from any onlookers. As fatigue takes over our bodies, the faces act as an indicator of the amount of energy we could be left with. It shows our level of functionality when we are in a team and the others can notice our capabilities.

#9: Infrequent blinking and eyes fixed on a particular thing shows they're probably focused

A focused facial expression tends to vary depending on the situation. If an individual is focused on a given task, they will have their eyes fixed on it. If the same individual is focused on a thought or idea, they tend to look upward with their eyes facing the side.

You may also notice that they blink once in a very long time. An interesting part about how focus is facially expressed is when a person twists their tongue and will move it from side to side. Many are not aware that they are doing this. The phenomenon is referred to as motor disinhibition whereby a bigger percentage of your brain's energy is dedicated to the task while the remaining little energy keeps the body stagnant.

#10: Head scratching with the eyes gazing in the eye may indicate confusion

When one is confused, he/she is unaware of what direction to take.

They have a couple of options choose from, all of which seem viable.

This is a state that can be expressed by the face. It is mostly characterized by the nose and forehead scrunched up and there may be an eyebrow which is higher than the other.

The lips of the confused person are also pursed together while the actual confusion tend to be seen around the eyes.

Confusion is an indicator that you lack some understanding and the expression itself comes about when the individual puts in more effort to properly understand the matter at hand.

Chapter 5
Managing Personal Facial Expression

Knowing how to read facial expressions is as important as knowing how manage the same. Managing your facial expression is a simple task that can have significant impact on your life and communication skills.

There are countless benefits that come with being able to manage your facial expression. You may want to surprise someone but you do not want it to show or you may have decided to tell a story from a given perspective due to reasons best known to you and you do not want the other person to detect that. This chapter shows you how you can manage your facial expressions.

1. Increase your conscious alertness

Be more careful that you do not send out the wrong message from your unconscious 'neutral' mind through awkward facial display. It is a common issue amongst human beings that they may not understand what to do with their faces. However, when you pay the right attention, you will be able to see beforehand what facial you have displayed and handle it in advance.

When you have a high conscious alertness, it means that you are able to change your interpretation of a situation immediately it takes place, therefore having an upper hand on the emotion and hence the resultant facial expression.

Conscious alertness is able to penetrate the fast process that triggers a facial expression so that you can short-circuit the whole process. One way to increase your conscious alertness is to live in the NOW rather than the PAST. Being in the present implies that when something happens, your whole mind is available to perceive it.

2. Know your face

To control your facial expressions, you must understand your face. You can do this by resting your face and taking a picture of it. If you were the other person, would you initiate a small talk with someone sharing your resting face? You can also know your face by standing in front of the mirror. Keenly look at that face, and even try making mimics of various situations like sad, happy or surprised to know how you would look like.

3. Take control of your face's muscles

Facial expressions are directed by the muscles in your face. When the brain sends a particular signal, it is these muscles that pick the signal and adjust accordingly.

Thus, you need to manage these muscles if you are to feel that you are managing your facial expression. One of the ways to do this is by learning how to wiggle your ears. Stand in front of the mirror and practice.

You may notice that you squint your eyes, raise the eyebrows or close and open the mouth several times. These are different facial muscles which you should learn to control. For example, when someone tells you something that is surprising but you do not come across as being surprised, try keep your eyes minimal because widely opened eyes will give you away.

4. Perform facial expressions while alone

Allow yourself some quality time in front of the mirror and exercise different facial expressions. Take note of the changes in your mood as you put on different facial expressions. Understand how the body would feel with a give facial look and how that changes when another look is worn. Synchronization of the body's emotions with your face is vital as it gives you an idea in advance of what a particular emotion would make your face look like.

The only goal for you to do is manage the two to be in line when you want to pass across a particular message.

For example, as you speak with someone, make sure that you maintain eye contact with them at all times. Whether you are saying something that you believe in or not, maintaining eye contact is a show of confidence in oneself, hence confidence in your words.

5. Relax the mouth
Frown-shaped pout or neutral lips tend to be less inviting. Thus, make sure your facial muscles are relaxed by simply maintain a small parting of your lips.

When your facial muscles are relaxed, a warm message is sent by your face and this facial expression is easier to manage. Furthermore, relaxed mouth turns up the corners of your mouth, making you look more appealing and approachable.

6. Visualize what you are talking about

In order to appear as though you mean what you are talking about, it is paramount that your facial expression matches your words. By visualizing what you are talking about, you essentially make pictures in your head that put some life into your words. As you speak, you connect to the image and focus on then translate that image into the appropriate facial expression. Facial expression that does not match the words being said delivers a mixed message.

7. Get feedback

Get someone you trust and ask them to make an evaluation of your face as you speak.

This should be done in privacy. Are there any habits that you may have but are unaware of them?
Is your facial expression expressive enough in association to what you speak?

Chapter 6
How to be a Pro at Reading Facial Expressions

Decoding people's facial expressions is one skill that you cannot afford to miss out. With such a skill, you get information about people which the average person wouldn't have. Very few individuals have this kind of skill. No wonder we have too many heartbreaks and broken deals. Remember that 80% of emotions are shown by the face. So, if you get to properly decode the facial expressions in advance, you will highlight behaviors that signal danger in the near future. This chapter takes you through the various ways in which you can become better at reading people's facial expressions.

#1: *Differentiate between observing and looking*

Most people look at others' faces, thinking they are observing them. Even though both observation and looking is done with the use of eyes, the two are completely different. They are mistakenly used to mean the other but that ought to change.

Looking is when you see others without the intent of getting to know more than what is visible to the eye. You do not try to derive meaning out of the actions done by others neither do you try to commit anything to the brain.

Observing has to do with seeing the actions performed by people and keeping the visions in mind so that you can make meaning out of them, posing questions. You perform deductions, that is, separating vital details from the unimportant ones, utilizing your careful observation to conclude.

Make sure that you know the two are different so that you do not waste time looking at people thinking you are observing them. In fact, in looking you will end up awkwardly staring others and it may even earn you a smack in the face.

#2: Be curious

For you to decode one's facial expression, you must have some form of curiosity towards him/her. It is this curiosity that drives you to dedicate your time observing them. It is human nature to pay attention to what interests them. If you develop negative attitudes towards others, chances are you may not observe them diligently. That calls for an effort on your part to prevent your feelings or emotions from getting in the way of your observation. Even if you do not like somebody but you still have to observe them, make sure that you keep the dislike at bay or else you will achieve nothing.

Identify something that you find to be intriguing about others and curiously purpose to exploit it further. Understand that we all learn from each other and so even if they appear to be different, appreciate that and continue observing them. Is there somebody you do not like but they still have friends who are so fond of them? Curiosity would drive you into wanting to know why they have the following despite you despising them. If you spot some differences between you and others, curiosity would lead you into wanting to know why the differences exists.

#3: Say NO to judgment

Being judgmental is the number one thing that will block you from making effective observation of people. When you judge others, you feed your brain with the wrong information and block it from getting facts. For a good people observer, neutrality is prioritized. Observations are free of personal feelings since such elements are comprised of biasness. When you involve prejudices, preconceived notions and personal feelings, you are not able to see what is there. You only get to see what you want to see. A good people observer knows how to ignore their personal feelings so that they can feed their brains with the right details for analysis.

To avoid being judgmental as you go about observing others, begin by taking a step back. Refrain from trying to enter into the other person's life and let them just be themselves. Do not try to make conclusions about whatever they do. Rather than thinking of a negative experience you had with them or saw them perform, see them for who they are – a person. If they drive a certain car, do not look at them in a certain way just because you associate the car with a particular social class. When you are neutral, you are able to see people clearly. The person driving a 'cheap car' may be building a multi-billion house just across the street. Your neighbor with an expensive car might have to work three jobs to pay for it.

#4: Stare more where possible

There is something about staring at people that makes you get finer details that had been previously concealed from your eyes. One of the ways to observe people is to stare at them and the things they like doing, but you must make sure you are not within the framework that might define you as being 'creepy.' We tend to encode more information from what the eyes sees as opposed to what is spoken or written. Stare as much as necessary for the eyes to pick relevant data and send it to the brain for analysis.

Staring at people can be a tricky engagement. Even from your own perspective, if you see somebody just staring at you, you will feel kind of awkward or may even want to react violently. Thus, your staring should be a purposeful stare but one that is concealed. If you can get your hands to videos involving such people and uploaded online, the better. You could lock yourself in a room and stare at the people in videos until you get what you are looking for. While in public, control the urge to stare to levels that let you get basic information.

#5: Avoid distractions

The reason as to why you may not perform a good observation is because you are distracted. As you go about your observation, a WhatsApp notification on your smartphone could force you to lose focus on what you were doing. The distractions are all over us, whether it's your to-do list, music or cell phones. The best way to focus on people observation is to eliminate these distractions.

Remove your headphones as you interact with other people. Allow yourself to hear the surrounding sounds and probably what others are saying (but do not appear to be eavesdropping). If you are watching a video that has the person whom you are observing, concentrate on it as you listen to any conversations held. Rather than watching mindlessly, pay attention. Think about what they wore and why they acted in a particular way.

Conclusion

Thank you again for downloading this book!
I hope this book was able to help you to learn how to analyze people.
The next step is to go ahead and build meaningful relationship and friendship with the new people analysis skills learned.

Finally, if you enjoyed this book, then I'd like to ask you for a favor, would you be kind enough to leave a review for this book on Amazon? It'd be greatly appreciated!

Thank you again and good luck!

www.ingramcontent.com/pod-product-compliance
Lightning Source LLC
Chambersburg PA
CBHW030737180526
45157CB00008BA/3213